Heat of the Moment

OTHER BOOKS BY THE AUTHOR

Verse booklets

Learning Not To Touch (Redbeck Press, 1998)
Reaching for a Stranger (Shoestring Press, 1999)

Verse Collections

Outstripping Gravity (Redbeck Press, 2000)
Exposures (Redbeck Press, 2003)
Taking Cover (Redbeck Press, 2005)
No Time for Roses (Salzburg Press, 2009)
Refuge (New Generation Press, 2012)
Here And Now (Severn Press, 2015)
Bridging The Gap (Severn Press, 2018)
Alive in Winter (New Generation Publishing 2023)

Narrative verse fantasy for younger readers

Wish (Thames River Press, 2012)
Rainbow (Thames River Press, 2012)
Woodsy (New Generation Press, 2014)

More information on the author's website:
www.michaeltolkien.com

HEAT OF THE MOMENT

-◆-

Michael Tolkien

New Generation Publishing

Published by New Generation Publishing in 2024

Copyright© Michael Tolkien 2024

First Edition

Paperback ISBN: 978-1-83563-261-1
Hardback ISBN: 978-1-83563-262-8

www.newgeneration-publishing.com

ACKNOWLEDGEMENTS

Some of these poems appeared in *Ambit* and in *Behind the Scenes Workshops*, a Leicestershire Literature Development project. *Elegy at Pantasaph* won second prize in the 2007 Bedford Open Poetry Competition and featured in *The Interpreter's House 37*.

Much is owed to members of *Inky Fish* for workshopping countless poems since 1994, particularly to Robert Hamberger and Pam Thompson whose detailed reading of this collection provided perspectives for its structure, content and text.

Thanks also to Gordon Braddy, former colleague, and to H. Lomas and J. Forth, poets and critics, who rescued several poems from being labored or obscure.

As ever the personal and professional support of Darin Jewell (Inspira Group Literary Agency) has been indispensable.

The author thanks the editors of *Poetry Salzburg* for publishing in 2009 the original, now remaindered edition of this collection, '*No Time for Roses*', and for granting permission for the poems to be republished by *New Generation Press**.

*(See further explanatory note in the Appendix)

COVER ILLUSTRATION

A painting by Rosemary Tolkien

CONTENTS

II PACKAGE... *Shots from a Package Deal*

III *JOHN'S EXCLUSIVES*

IV *UNFOLDING*

For Rosemary

'...He sulks, snorts, preaches new art forms...But there's enough space for all, new and old: why do we have to wrestle?'

Chekov: *The Seagull*, act iii

♠

'It may come to the notice of posterity... that this our age ran wild in the quest for new ways to be new.'

Robert Frost: Introduction to *King Jasper,* Poems of E.A. Robinson, 1935

I

INHERITANCE

WAYSIDE STORES

They've straightened the road,
felled and levelled
to carve out desirable plots.

Old Stores in hatched gilt
swings from a teak frame.
Palings guard gold Leylandi
shorn to match selected grass.
Tread gravel through spiked
gates to stone porch, carefully.

***

We shopped here fifty years ago.
Mrs Ricks was fat, and had a weak,
kind heart, kept us alive on bargains,
excused me to Mum and Dad as
only a boy, while she scissored
extra fatty bacon and slipped me
a tuppenny bar for the walk.

I stumble back up a flinty track.
Two chestnuts overhang
piecemeal red brick
called *'Blossom's'* after her
and them. The door clanger
drags her smile and swollen ankles
to the counter.

INHERITANCE*

Grandma revered George Grove,
musicologist and distant forbear.
She left me his christening cup to grace
my piano lid. Her curt sing-song voice
still makes it shine apart from fancy
bowls, spoons and napkin rings.

This plate-silver fluted chalice set
on a circular fan, its neck
a shank of missing jewels must never tarnish
or leave its print in dust.

Someone floored it at a drinks party.
Behold the blood of the righteous! I said.
A dented rim adds lustre to a goblet.
And Grandma's eyes were on me again
in withering disbelief. No way
to behave if I'd wanted her to play
for me, her angry need to please at war
with arthritic fingers. How she'd flicker
in Grove's sheen, petite and elegant,
turning staves loaded with heavy black
to rampaging Beethoven who rattled
the metronome and all her fine-bone china.

*Note on Page 82

MUSIC LESSON

Prelude in C minor

Morning break in endless May.
'You're not playing. Leave us alone.'
But I'm not staking my claim.
From muffled piano deep inside the school
Bach sidles *cantabile* into hot air's
squeals and laughter. My feet stuck
on a field scuffed into baked mud, I stare
through yew hedge arch willing these notes
to pour from wide-tiled entrance hall,
dip and soar like a flight of swallows.

How can that stern periwigged Master I call
Auld Lang Bark, who stares cross-eyed
from my bedroom wall, leap about in sixths,
make perky calls and answers, turn fun and games
upside down in flowing waters, steal in mid play
a heart that longs for parts that fit,
only to ache for what's beyond?

And Mrs Birkbeck keeps him at it
with those bent-tipped smoker's fingers,
her black mop head and its aloof,
bird-beady eyes behind thick specs.

As for my piano hour, one creak of her corset
turns keys to pitfalls, baits every bar with poison.
Now she stops my breath, turns my legs to jelly,
makes Bach pitch simplicity beyond reach
while slimy Parnell steals my playground girl.

ROAD PUBLIC LIBRARY 1950

'Wait on a bench and take Trolley Bus numbers
or come in and make sure you behave.'
Clear choices from Grandpa Griffiths,
though when his duodenal quietened down
he'd begin: 'OK then, chief. How about it?'
Rain might drive me to follow him under stone portals
and through the many-windowed swivel door
with its polished kick-proof brass plates.
Some roundabout, if I could keep it reeling!

First get past a row of staff specs glinting
from their oak fortress. For the worst of them
I found edible names: *Mister Acid Drop,*
Marge Mince Pie, Sylvie Smart Tart.
They hated library users. At me they fired
a special glare. *No ticket! Guilty!* And they
could play with the serious toys of their trade.
I coveted those roller calendars, date stamps,
drawers of coloured cards, fat maroon ledgers.

Strikes, Russia, big football took him into
Papers and Atlases. While grandpa stood at
the *Mail,* sacred text wired to its tall lectern,
I pored over a giant book of maps. Coastlines
drew me creatures: Iceland, my ragged sheep,
Dyfed, the snarling hound. South America's
triangle I longed to trace, crayon its countries,
shade the Andes, copy names that sang to me.
'Pencils here! You'd be out on your ear, my lad!'

Quietly now along towering blocks of colour-
coded binding with gilded titles and index numbers.
Good for hide-and-seek, though I dare not lose
grandpa with his cross-patterned leather bag,
crafty sleuth hunting down unread thrillers.
Four a week he devoured, along with Woodbines
and strong mints, sniffing at jokes or enigmas.
O to join stray sparrows in that unreachable
cupola, my legs dangling above the hush and fuss.

SPREE

In the outfitters two 'good old boys'
hunt for bargains, talking last night's telly,
some bird showing her tits for no good reason.
Dick lurches towards the till with socks
and sweaters, jolts me as I queue for dry cleaning.
Apologises grimly. Left his stick behind.
But listen to Alf. 'Shirts in the window's
cheaper. Mind if I climb in?' Assistant
Liz hasn't heard, or has she? 'Hope
I won't lose you customers, clambering over
your display. Won't do my flasher turn!
Got any easycare polywhatsit stuff?
Get your shirts seen to regular then Dick?
Pound a time.' 'Too much,' says Dick.
'Don't mind doing some ironing myself.'
'Not man's work!' grunts Alf, swivelling
his bum off the ledge with two square-patterned,
cotton-rich shirts he slaps on the counter.
'Shouldn't do it. All this bloody housework!
We'll become a nation of fairies.'
'Lot to think about there,' I say to Liz,
who murmurs about a bit of male help
around the place being no bad thing.

BUTCHER'S GHAZAL

I'm Bob standing behind my cleaned-off slab.
Reckon my ruddy cheeks recommend my meat.

The mean ones come dragging their feet
over the cobbles. They'll take scraps for meat.

But here's another with a quid or two to spare.
Try and fob him off with a chunk of stringy meat.

Now there's Mavis Porter who loves a bit of fat.
Nice slice of wrapped topside. That's her meat.

Best pork sausages are Charlie Calder's life line.
Goes to show how oats and barley pass for meat.

Pigs trotters do well. Good cheap fare, they reckon.
So be it if bone and gristle taste like meat.

O I've got prime steak and best loin of pork,
and those who know me know it's no easy meat.

'New season lamb chops, please.' 'Here we are,
Patsy.' ('Bone and grease with a sliver of meat!')

I've been at this game for twenty years and more.
Doubt if anyone's better at cheating with meat.

UNCOVERED

I kill time in *Biography.*
The dead and dying rub shoulders,
invite us in with gaudy spines.

Alexander the Great leans on
Anne Boleyn. Prise Austen from Auden
only to find her swamped in coffee-table tat,
next to *BRIGITTE*, a photographic study,
And God Created Woman, tall and glossy.

I try *BARDOT* by Glenys Roberts, weighty,
well-researched, dedicated *To My Mother.*
Sex symbol bursts her bonds chapter
by no-nonsense chapter to burgeon
into breathing woman. Ballet girl, cover
pout to film debut, off-screen lover,
dumping it all for animal rights.

Brighid, 'high one', fire goddess, star
I haven't seen on screen, who never
stirred a dream, here you are sealed up
in palm-greased long-life plastic wrap.
Your dust-jacket face asks *Why me?*
What next? It's framed in milky
tangerine behind gilt-lined wrought iron—
bedstead or bric-a-brac?—one bar curving
to the shape of your left cheek.

LIMBO

Was it time to end the story
he'd tried to rearrange
with cool evasion?

She turned to him as if to ask
how far she should trust
in all this,

too true to what she felt
not to send out sparks
of tortoiseshell.

Those flecks in her eyes!
he found himself thinking.
Butterflies

always longing to alight
on warmth, and so easily
taken in.

GROUNDED

After baggage reclaim
yellow signs hustled them
to exit from each other,
but they stopped their trollies
to take turns in the loo.
'I'm wet. I need to,'
she said, though soon out,
grumbling about the queue.

Words he heard another way
that night when stacked planes
circled with a joke of hers
that must have passed him by
somewhere over Europe.

It was when all of a sudden
they'd held hands, gently
kissed, and she'd shown him
another plane floating below
in silver innocence, saying
with a smile in her eyes:
'It's so good to fly!'

PROPORTIONS

In no mood
for symmetries and verdigrised
sculptures of the Ancien Régime,
the tourist leans heavily
against a bronze equine leg
and feels how, after all,
passions that seem to lurk
under your clothes
won't become the stuff of history.

All that vision and design:
backdrop for one who fears
a need to love, whose mouth's allowed
to play its own tricks,
who slams the lid tight
on what screams to be heard until
it dwindles to an echo
from far down some
long-forgotten corridor.

FACE OF POWER: 1400 BC

A golden mask is what they made of me.
Time refines better than fire. Now
I'm pure gold; my words untarnished.

Listen to my golden words, though you can't
tune in to the notes of my gilded tongue,
whose riches no subject heard me mouth.

Of course you *will* attend to royal
Mycenaean pride crafted into
fine strokes and measured etchings.

Feel this voice vibrate in my beard's
hatched lines, my high, brushed eyebrows
that overarch this golden map of me,

depicting my perfect command of who I am.
Trace here my rugged kingdom: mountains,
ravines, pastures, its unseen running waters.

Eyes locked in perfect ovals, I'm ready
for another move no one can guess,
steadfast before ranks of hostile spears,

unmoved by the seductive usurper
who knows more than is good for him.
Gold-mouthed, I prescribe poison

to defend him from himself. I'm praised
for purging my golden realm.
Some kings are sacrificed. Not me.

DIDO & ÆNEAS*

I

Golden-tongued spokesman
you touched Dido with your tale
of unjust exile.

O Sidonian
so moved to fatal mercy
by Anchises' son

your last free words told
warriors to eat and drink.
Then lust devoured you.

He has charmed Carthage,
left its queen twice widowed, chanced
his cause to the waves.

II

In Underworld woods
you flit towards him, a thin
pale moon veiled in cloud.

His regrets meet eyes
blank and hard as flakes of flint,
your Sphinx lips wire-tight.

Is he here to twist
the blade you took to your heart,
relight your pride's pyre?

Too late he recalls
idle soldiers, destiny,
the first off-shore wind.

*Note on Page 83

25

PANACEAS

1

Take **The Three Bears.**
No one cares who they were,
these furry cave-dwellers who chose
to live in a little house in the middle of a wood.

Recent research reads **Bores**.
All made to measure, nothing
left to chance. Sticklers for routine,
they spoke in formulae, one by one.

No house, no wood.
Buried in a well-roofed dugout
behind ranks of tall, dark palings,
they shut out the slightest doubt.

And Blondie found a door unlocked.
The world was her oyster.
She walked in, smashed up
others' lives and sneaked off scot-free.

2

Drive off the suburban road
into a narrowing tunnel of evergreens
lit up with candelabra.

Spiked tendrils reach out
from tangled undergrowth to claw
your comfortable shell.

And beyond those black fingers ahead?
Thwack- Zing- Riddle-riddle
shriek the gathering birds.

3

Edgy? Not quite yourself?
Make it straight Darjeeling!

Pour tanned gold
through well-stained sieve
onto sliced lemon.

When the pot sighs
tilt it, thumb on lid,
until it dribbles dry.

Make sure your lemon
floats, surging from side
to side in the heat.

Feel bitter nectar
take you by the throat.

EVENING IN A SCULPTURE GARDEN

1

Lawn-locked Starfish

You wonder whether my eight striped,
glazed horns are hollow or stuffed
with clay, edible tissue, membrane.

Run your hand up one of my ridges
until you reach the tip. What's in there?
Venom? Perceptions? Micro-chip memories?

You presume I lie on this shorn turf
day and night. Suppose dawn moves
me a millimetre, rocking from spike to spike?

Admit my glitter tempts you
to maim me for a souvenir.
Why not settle for the status quo?

How does my maker feel, leaving me here,
the whole bristling mass of me alive,
pulsing through dream green seas?

2

Blank Pages, Open Minds

... Be thou, Spirit fierce,
My spirit! Be thou me, impetuous one! (Shelley: *Ode to the West Wind*)

Shelley, your spirit hovered,
hazed round objects posing in light or shade,
    flew with words that longed
to hold and surpass the moment. You soared
among thoughts set free like wayward leaves in a gust,
    swirling round to embrace
stone, iron, woven wire and wood, last flowers,
     greenery so crystalline
in low-slanted sun after weeks of rain.

    Astral seer, you winged
one writer through gnat-dance curtains to galaxies
    of spheres and orbits, our pied
globe a fitful pinhead looped by a speck of moon.
    His universe took fire
from light-catching discs that must have alighted
    among branches of oak.

Another you sent headlong through woods,
    unshackled his mind,
true to impulse as your West Wind.
    Exhibits dismembered him,
parts of his anatomy seen afresh.
    You made him breathe
through many valves, feel one in all.

3

Aspire

Beast slouched in camouflaged rest,
or loops of embedded emerald snail?
Were these wide green spirals gritty earth
swirled into three interwoven scarps,
to be stitched tight with rough–cut grass,
dock, plantain? Why do more well up,
smaller and steeper in the mind's eye?

Surprisingly gentle slope winds you
to a top you'll somehow never reach.
Go back. Try once more. That upward
swivel lures you with its long, slow ascent
to detachment, so spongy you're lifted
barefoot towards a receding goal
beyond the silky meadow's straw-pale mat.

Reluctantly down on the beaten track
watch one man raise his brown castle,
bristling green to him as he dumps load
after load, rakes, steps back to gauge the grade,
wiping away grime that blinds him to the odds.
Has he buried more than sweat below
these carted tons, made an ageless barrow?

4

Simply Jurassic

Grizzled chunk planted
  on clipped roadside green where five ways meet,
flawed key or corner stone,
  or too prized to be hewn and honed
to hand-sized blocks?

I watch your millions of years driven past
  by those the clock drives,
your barnacle skin palmed without a thought.
  Few finger your cryptic grooves.
It's not only kids you tempt to jump
  from your weathered crust
or clear you with a yelling leap.

Comfortably square old timer
  I speak like this before some know-all
splits us up by telling me
  who he thinks you are.

UNDER THOMAS HARDY'S SKIN

1

*A Century on at Aldeburgh**

i

Expectant hours trundled us once again
   East along a winding seaward road that plunged past
Flint-faced walls and hallowed tower's disdain
   To meet embracing blue that shouted *Back at last,*
      Are you, with your lovely woman!

Familiar shifting shingle underfoot
   Lit by October's last low slanting light,
We outpaced vacant strollers setting foot
   From the comfort of cars, blind to the sight
      Of a lover with his lively woman.

ii

Alone then and treading stones among
   Springy twitch, untouched by seas for years untold
Yet buffed by feet that shuffled along
   Or told like ours of a purpose to unfold.

Traversing well-worn ground, some would say.
   Flowing talk and locked hands may have brought us back,
But up ahead we found a surer way,
   Like breakers new-shaped with each surge back.

*Note on Page 83

2

Sweet Recompense

How novelty set you aquiver
When her smile dawned.
O she'll be all to me!
And not once did you waver
Or wonder at the cost.
Stock that seemed its own supplier
Drawn on day in day out.
You and she rode ever higher.
And nothing ran out.

How and where could she stay?
Envious eyes are watchful.
O stare and lay us bare!
How could that sort learn to play
Harmonies like yours?
Together all those breathless hours
What obstacles remained?
After-sighs said heaven's yours,
Yours to be regained.

3

Last Testament Too Late

When I am gone and have no further say,
If there's a god minded to have his way,
He'll have no man or woman countermand my will,
That I'll be laid abed to rest asleep and still
    Among the unsung,
    One passing bell rung
To lower me beside the dead who've had their fill.

Let them not burn this heap of flesh and bone,
Urn-incarcerate its cinders under flag stone,
Roof them away from rain, wind and shine.
I won't be made a monument like some fine
    Contrite knight
    Paying for heaven's light
In a cavernous vault of his own design.

Those I know would gladly overrule the private man,
Inflate what's left of me to make a public talisman
With city pomp and pantomime, rip some part
Of me away and grass it in to satisfy my heart,
    Deluding the rude
    Who watch in mournful mood
That I am bedded whole as at my faltering start.

*Note on Page 83

WRITERS WANDER

Strolling downhill in a loose gaggle,
we emerge from high-hedged lanes
and flinch at the glint of glass-still
reservoir, suddenly small
before such wide-armed presence.

Dream up from clay-coated bed
    brown river bubbling slowly
round sheep,
      heads among winter mangle, past barley
  silk-headed, splashed with poppy blood,
and farmsteads waiting to be felled.

Breathe all breaths
    drawn on that wide air.
Crawl on clogged tracks and tear
    through opencast mine of slime.

Time and water...
        Water and time…

And so we stand at the mirror's verge
where some watch web-foot birds sail,
talk of their pride and how they settle
politics with shrieks or snide assaults.

A girl in yellow flower print dress
joins us late with cup, saucer and biscuits,
squats cross-legged on twisted reeds,
drinks, eats, scribbles, pauses
like a taut bird, listening to phrases.

Where are we? What's this dazzling waste?

INNER TUNING

You sweat steeply up over marsh and rock
    to the unroofed railway halt.
Fog of fine rain chills you to the bone,
    draws a deadening wall across
mountains scored and etched with earth's upheavals.
    Your soul shivers. Should you wander
further, hoping for bearings without the diversion
    of glacier, scree, dream summit?

Listen! An unknown bird, *mezzo piano*,
    persists with unanswered signal,
suggests steep-clinging forests far below.
    Maybe! Maybe! Or is it bounced
and muffled into what you think you'd like to hear?
    Such motifs seep into the soul
when baffling mist begins to strip it bare.

Your tentative boot rests on a glistening rail.
    The last train's white eye
shrieks round a rock face its lights unveil.
    You must attend to this wary
racked descent. Is it destined to carry
    you below thickening cloud,
crawling back to where the soul is wrapped away
    on a wide, distracting highway?

CUTTING ACROSS

Statistics are made from other
people. Yet at these unboarded
rails, your path from stile to stile,
you pause and think *Red for Danger.*

No signal. Just piebald
horses grazing sedge-spiked meadow
yellow with toxic ragwort.

Creep over creaking ballast
without a wasted breath, ready
for that hissing ventriloquy
of wheels two miles away.

Railway! So reassuring!
Our orderly, unruffled
trundling of trucks and coaches
along well-groomed track.

Isenbahn, Chemin de Fer, Ferrocarril
are buckled down to pierce the land
with crisp iron. Steel tyres
slice along burnished girders
precise as a guillotine.

BETWEEN VILLAGES

Walk due south through spring hectares.
Under sliced hedges celandines sprout
yellow leaves and droop. Hybrid daffs
once spaced along the verge, dangle,
unsure which way to face.

Briefly the road dips between
shoulders of a lopped railway arch.
I blunder into bushes for a pee.
A white high heel glints up at me.
I shrink from its story.

East, a desirable windmill, upmarket-white.
South, a spire tip sinks out of sight
and a rusting dutch barn kneels on two legs.
West, houses plaster slopes that wall in
a wide experiment of rolled stripes.

Keep-Off country. Miles of invested
powder tightly bedded down, field margins
poisoned into livid weed-free strips.
Timed scarers mounted like mini cannons
blast as if to fell advancing infantry.
And not a wing or bobbing tail in sight
till my ballistic head explodes a shower of doves.

RADIOACTIVE*

Idaho
Gale blunders down my chimney into
radio report on dumping cover-ups,
howls along to a horror march that fades
to Idaho's governor, quietly defiant
in this vacant roar. Sub-fleet garbage
won't fester above their finest aquifer.
His M60 tanks are out and armed.
A state trooper stands between rails, loud-
hails guards on their armoured caboose:
Move that thing when you're told to.

Nevada
My radio crackles off station and returns
to waste canisters about to nestle
ten thousand years in a ten-mile tunnel
deep inside Yucca Mountain.
Nameless voice, matter-of-fact:
　*virtual nuclear attack... dark clouds
　　on our borders... interim storage
　　　equals permanent disaster.*

Texas
Gusts suck at my doors. Will grid cables clash
and short the whole county? I search for
pocket torch to rumours of a radiated
watercourse below the Texan panhandle's
green horizons. A bony farmer talks cancer
as if recalling a career, dryly sketches in
bulbous cattle and kids with no hair or fingers.
Crowbars strike my roof, set gutters
moaning. Window ledges snarl in protest.

*Note on Page 83

BEGUILED BY

creation

When it first cooled into something
appetising, I hoped they'd sing
about it, feed, rest.
They devoured it and forced
me back to the melting pot.

adventure

From its deep pram
the child's hand clutches
a first coverlet of snow.
Avalanches later, no
hospital will hold out hope.

sex

To feel the first layers,
trace shapes of warmly-kept
secrets, ease a forbidden strap,
skies him miles before
he plummets back to earth.

travel

Winter's first brochures kindle
our dream with shots of olive
bodies flowering in primal blue.
But after all it's still us,
harassed and taking off late.

II

PACKAGE

SHOTS FROM A PACKAGE DEAL

1

On a balcony table filter tips
pressed down anyhow into

a white ashtray that matches an empty
cup and saucer. Still life shot.

All these new leases of life kissed
by a sun that never stops smiling.

2

In shallow water children play
their many selves. One idea's
as good as another. Pool cues
for Olympic rowing on a latex
whale, or a shoot out. Then let's
get the girls or somersault like dolphins.

Parents ignore them or yell some half-
meant warning. Bask over bottled beers,
moan about this year's tariffs and nights
trailing the kids along just because
Mum and Dad wanted a quiet Christmas.

Refreshing in all this heat
to meet others who feel the same.

3

'Christmas Eve tomorrow, Dad.
Can't wait!'

Grunts from the pool table.
Flip-flops shuffle under the weight
of a hangover that won't shift.

What a ref! They'd lost last night.
On satellite at McReady's.
Leather-padded tavern, *the* place
to take wife and kids for big games.
Good food, bottles of the best.
And the only British crisps in town.

          'Dad! Do you think Santa will make it
all the way here?'

' `Course he will. We'll leave him
a bottle of Brown and some Havanas.'

4

A very large person from Blackheath
persuades his new-found half-pissed
poolside buddies he's seen and done
the lot, which means anything worth
their while. Con artist, poet or both?
Either way he's a pro who deserves
tiptop hype and a frontline print run.

O he knows how to step on the word-flow,
rev the voice to mark up twists and turns,
brakes hard or soft for those teaser
pauses, runs twice round the block
when you think you know where you are.

Just enough props, *dramatis personae*
a nice mix of wits and clowns. *The* outing,
some mates, birds beefy or stringy who
might have wanted it but *we* couldn't stop,
sand, all-night bars. Talk about *laugh*!
And they all do, raucous, falling about,
hamming up the rôle he's given them.

5

O for that evening moment!
High-pressure showers spattering,
clothes slipped off hangers,
high heels precarious on mock marble,
plastic swish of tailored palms
neatly spaced down terraces,
lights coming on like heavenly bodies
by some law unknown to physics,
throaty roar of half-hourly bus
to where it all happens after dark
and blurs into the last star.

Twilight rolls up yesterday's
UK papers read again to make it
sunnier with bad news and storms,
while far-off chained Alsatians
ho-ho at alarms shrieking into life
as power trips and surges
after sudden dusk.

Mobile loudspeakers bring heaven nearer
at tonight's *Club Fantastico*, strafe
apartment blocks like automatics,
and stir from its balcony trance
the Chestnut Tan that fortifies
tropical dusk with lager, chaser
and another cigar, as *HOTEL GRANDE*
starts to wink flirtatiously at *MIRANDA*
who glares back in mint-green.

6

Leave behind threats of minus 5,
Prime Minister's lowest rating,
a slow Christmas with High Street
profits down (though turkeys were buoyant)
and share poolside worst-scenarios.

Thirteen hour delays and foreigners
getting 'preferential'. Ops that clashed
with holiday plans. Day trip
when broken glass sliced an artery.
Greedy locals who hiked up prices
and drove us to try here for a change,
to share such demanding lives
in the glow and airy twinkling
of chlorinated surfaces.

Change position or buy
a round if you like; the future's out
as are *How*, *When,* or *Why*,
unless exchange rates oscillate.

Now is a row of bottles with gold-foiled
tops, opening the way to another night
that waits, dependable as clingfilm.

A snort just above the surface
as you rise from the umpteenth dive
to twinkling bubbles of sun and
DON'T DRIVE ME TOO FAR, BABY:
I'LL NEVER FORGET YOU...' 'Get away
from that bloody edge, Stacey, or
I'll give you one to remember...'
Then chips as we watch the parascender's
flaming chute top the twelfth storey and
☻ ☻ ☻ PLEASE TAKE INTO THE POOL NO INFLATABLES
☼☼☼
Plunges after a six-hour roast,
spluttering from the amphibian
who desperately needs aluminium steps
and its Polar Bear towel.
Then at SEVENTEEN FORTYFIVE
you've had your quota of UVA or B.
It's getting harder to avoid the shadows.
Bar musack's fading, shutters are half down...

III

JOHN'S EXCLUSIVES

♠

For Anne Beresford

NEWS FOR THE PEOPLE OF SYCHAR

The woman said: "Sir, give me this water so that I may stop being thirsty..."

John: 4:15

There's a Jew by the well, thirsty enough
to ask a Samaritan for a drink, let alone
a woman with tainted pots. But somehow
he takes me as he finds me, insists on
how he can give me flowing water,
more alive than what comes out of a well,
though he hadn't so much as a cracked cup
to his name. Did he think himself better
than our father Jacob who tapped that deep
spring centuries back? No answer. Just that
  his brand of water really quenches thirst,
  like having the source of life inside you.

Why not take him at his word? All I get
is *First fetch me your husband.* No use
fobbing him off. A complete stranger
who tells me I've got through five men;
matter-of-fact, though, not wagging his finger.
So then he's a prophet, and I tell him to look
at that hill where our folk always worshipped,
and what business have Jews like him
to say shun it and make for Jerusalem?
  He says there's a revelation at hand.
  It won't matter where we meet our father.

Did he mean a Messiah who'll sweep old ways
aside, make everything clear, lead us?
Casual and calm as if I'd tried to guess
his name, he says I'm talking to the Holy One
we all expect. That's when his cronies arrive
with food and drink. If looks could kill!
But they say nothing, and I make off
without my pots, my mouth dry from defying
      him, and yet his words begin to
      quench a thirst I never knew I had.

TAKEN

'He that is without sin among you, let him first cast a stone at her.'

John **8**:7

Out of sight behind the garden shed
we stack the Sanhedrin's cure
for adultery. Brick ends, shaled
limestone, hammer-proof cobbles,
concrete lumps that glitter with pebbles.
Think of it smashing into skin and bone
for having the nerve to stretch and flex.

~ A ~

The one who refused to turn stones
into loaves sits in the temple teaching
a spellbound crowd. Jealous officials
wheel me in to use against him:
engaged woman who's taken a lover.
I'm no decoy primed to snare him
with my wiles. They've tricks enough.
"Master, Moses tells us to stone her."
Outcast if he snubs the old law,
up before the Romans if he doles out
death. And that will start a riot.

Judges are supposed to sit, ponder
and pass sentence. He rises, stoops
with his back to us all, and writes
on dusty marble with the finger
he should be pointing at me.
All that dust raised by Scribes
and Pharisees nit-picking over laws!

"Which of you are witnesses, pure
in motive, perfect in reputation? She's
yours. Throw first, and make it straight."
They watch him write. ***Rouse, arouse.***
Assent, consent…
I notice the clenched fists of young
Zealots, silenced, white with rage,
having to follow the Elders out.
Has he aped their word games
and shown what filthy minds lurk
below those white-washed manners?

~ Ω ~

No more hairs to split. The play's over.
You stand before her with the skies for judge.
She's uncondemned, has nothing to say,
and you're no rabbi to probe with words of fire.
Even the thought of hurling rubble
makes you weak at the knees.

THE POOL BETHZATHA*

*...in these porticoes lay a multitude of invalids...Jesus knew that
one man had been lying there a long time...*

John **5**: 2-6 [adapted]

Left at the five-arched waters
daily for thirty-eight years
he's derelict among sinners
who grope for the best place
to await a healing ripple.
Even on the Sabbath an Angel
might offend and stir the surface.

Jesus is footsore but treads firmly
through the Sheep Gate intent
on his offering for 'Trumpets',
finds himself held by water
shining on withered limbs strewn
over a basket litter, a face
furrowed by habits of failure.

He reads there the Jews' uneasy
patience in the wilds beyond
Jordan, eight and thirty years
starved of grace between Kadesh-
barnea and the brook Zered.
Still festering on the brink
after centuries of guidance.

'Do you still want to be healed?'
A strong voice searches the cripple
who cannot even crane his head
to see above the dusty garment.
'First come first served. Who'll lift
me in when the angel draught
brushes that cistern and starts a rush?'

He hears an intake of breath,
then like trumpets blasting down
the walls of Babylon, that voice:
'Time for you to get up and walk.'
And picking up his pallet, light
as a bunch of reeds, he breaks
the Sabbath with his wholesome arms.

*Note on page 83

IV

UNFOLDING

THE FOUR OF US

Mornings we open the curtains to ask the ash
what's in store, how the skyline looks.
Suppose we kept them drawn. Would it wonder
why we'd left it to itself? A closer
look shows two trees, once hedgerow
saplings that threw in their lot together,
one bending slenderly away
to invite the other's knotted limb.

Heaving away from another gust does Ash
make anything of that? As for its moods:
what moods? Only as many as ours.
How did we feel when one guest
peered into a windswept dawn and said:
That tree will need some attention?
We joined it in looking away.

WORDS AND PAINT

I watch you paint a window scene,
lost to time and place as if unruffled
care for shape and colour is all
that will ever be required of you.
Light-hearted though when you fall
short and nothing fits, as if it's just
a game, until at last the whole begins
to breathe. And glancing at those limpid
leaves and folded fields I feel your voice
brush me like a current of air:
gentle reminder that I'll follow any
scent to douse the hunt for words.

Hours later I've tidied papers, paid
bills, walked miles, and not a word
in the net, while you still make
good every nagging defect, re-tint
each curtain crease with shafts of light
and shade. Tomorrow I'll fix a word
for shaping out of dross, a *god* word
for making stillness come alive.

EASTER VIGIL

Witness the Great Candle kindled
from paraffin-soaked charcoal,
incensed in the bitter wind,

reedy chants blown apart
or swallowed by traffic hell-bent
on scurrying past this flimsy beacon

leading us away from night, sharing
its fire till we are lights that fill
the stripped vault we left in darkness.

You and I have been in a cavern,
carrying your weight of cancer,
waiting for those searing beams

to cleanse you. More than ever
side by side we kiss in peace
as Light scours a way ahead.

DISARMED

You are suddenly all the dearer
when I hear about a loved reporter
gunned down at random in Somalia.
You safe at home yet praised by a soldier.

On stinking dust-ridden days after
all-night missions she'd always ask
how others felt and knowing she wouldn't falter
made them equal to yet another risk.

I never saw her face and didn't hear
her voice; but like you she was one of few
who heal and give life by being there.
Now she's gone we're all somehow
more exposed: our horizon's undermined
and shadows are less sharply defined.

FROM A BENCH AT INTERLAKEN

White-blue of wide rapid Aare reflects
no park tree shade or towering scree.
Too icy and heedless to lull me through
an hour away from you. My eyes

plunge and surface on the far sunlit bank
where couples stroll, kids run rings round
parents, cyclists float, and suddenly
you that can't be you with your easy
unhurried walk, head leant forward,
hair spreading in the breeze, each leg's
backward thrust too lovely to be flung
away, cool in loosely undulating
stripes and flowers, your carrier hot
from streets ablaze with summer fashion.

This you who should be you holds me.
Shimmering vaguely through a gauze
of pathside shrubs, lost behind a boat house,
splashed by shadows. If only to turn across
the last bridge and being near become less
than you and all the more to look forward to.

FULL COVERAGE

Consulting your doctor about HRT
and a bruised finger was mostly
a long wait when every glossy featured
sexpertese. Smiley poses with real life
accounts of who likes what and when.

'To learn or unlearn?' you ask, laughing
at the hoax that smart talk makes anything
bigger and better. And after a late shift
wrung you dry, while my evening
hardened into night without respite,
such tips and chat jingle like shackles
beside our tenderness. No tracks
mark our discoveries. As ever
we arrive without a chart.

HEAT OF THE MOMENT

Into tea table talk of five
overloaded minds wanders
a small black cat, bright
with delight in being alive,
while hunched over ginger cake
and lapsang souchong, we make
a meal of Romantic pleasure-
pain agonies. Such relief
in its glossy coat and fierce
undemanding eyes! My chance
to turn away from listening to
Rachmaninov damned or praised,
I bend down as if to greet
that friend I always seem to
spot in seething foreign squares.
Purring as a matter of course,
with a golden glance it leaves me
tingling from a touch of silky
spine to curl up by the empty
black stove. Immaculate
matching swirl of fireside cat.

PAY LATER

After fifty years you speak out,
your tongue Holy Spirit flame;
you sing from your soul's core
longing to sear the old man's
dithering fear of a god
who tots up every rite and broken
rule, paving the way to hell
with all those Sunday duties missed.
Oh but as children we were told....
Then after eight decades tortured
by that mean-minded god,
he harks back to childhood
only to tighten his own noose.

You tell him *your* god's no
accountant, no wielder of lashes,
waits to be found and embraced.
And something shines on him
brief as winter sun from under
a day's cloud, too low, too late.
His tightly packed hellfire
out-burns your loving words.

SAFELY TO PICCADILLY STATION*

We might be piling into any taxi,
heaving luggage, fumbling for seatbelts
until I see a loop of sacred beads
dangling from the driver's mirror, one
for each of God's hundred and eight names.
Dark emerald necklace secured through
a fruit stone with a tufted knot, bucks
and sways to gears, brakes, sudden turns.

As the glass opens for our fare I ask,
though I know: 'Is that a japamala?'
His look says *What else? Why not?*
I tell him mine came from Puttaparthi.
He corrects my accent syllable
by syllable, repeats the name
with an inward smile, and shuts
himself away to queue for work.

*Note on Page 83

UNFOLDING

Up here we've put the *Eternal Shoot* on hold,
embracing moor, stray sheep, golf course,
patchwork valley in a loving sweep. You brush
through forty-five million years of ice and fire
in minutes. I swear I'll never club hard
little balls in search of eighteen shaven holes.
Bright summer couples carry their clutter and vision
down a spur of sun-parched bracken. The land
palpitates to itself. Muscles tighten
at the ninth. You ache from rock under
sheepshorn grass. I shoulder a rucksack
lighter for our ruminating lunch. Think
how it all converges. Somehow a finer
symphony for being so rarely grasped.

MENDIPS ON A WET EVENING

Leaving high-hedged lanes we feel
soft rain lick us, soak our scalps.
We grope uphill over shelf after shelf
of coarse grass. Why do farmers say
cattle *pick it down* over winter?
Mist numbs us. Fences, bushes, trees
never so stunted appear too soon,
play look-alike to show we're out
of our minds to come among them.

What makes us abandon known bearings
to labour feet first with muffled sight
into a stew of hill-clinging cloud?
We trip over stiff sedge disguised
as turf, slither on hoof-churned mud,
and feel the indifference of cows
suckling calves, supercilious
sheep who pee us off scent just
in case, then graze on unruffled.

Damp air curls your hair and rolls back
time. You're so young and your hand
so firmly in mine I must calculate
our way without a single fault,
bring you back below these leering
silhouettes, avoid the fear
and stumbling of a detour.

BELONG

In a fold between grass slopes,
red-brown cattle rested,
giant mole hills of Rutland earth.
We watched them wade deep in green
to graze, bucking calves overlooked
with unruffled chewing.

Far above, the crown of a by-road
gleamed, or was it a washed track
where carts clattered and drovers yelled?
A jeep and trailer top the slope
in a flurry of red dust.

***

Weeks later we find their dung
like shaled limestone, pitted by starlings.
Did missing them make this *Nowhere*
feel like *Somewhere*? Or had something
drawn them here? A woodpecker
laughs and pigeons clap away.

Faint paths merge. One bites
    hard to reach old railway gates.
Two gnarled, uprooted hawthorns cling
    together, flowering pink and white over
weathered rock. Its russet water
    spills into a stream that spreads a crackling ford,
then tunnels under eaves of alder.

Eastwards, open fields sink to sedge,
  narrow to a copse that blunts
winds honed on bare hills beyond.

Surely a hollow to settle or defend,
  a place to begin or end,
and yet we find no ruins, feel no ghost.

Perhaps like cattle we're more at rest
  where nothing's been planned or lost.

HAUNT

anywhere that might be there
   and wind-ruffled wader bird chorus
      pipe-trills back rusted, flaking boats askew
         on mud banks, salt-
            secreting bladder plants
               wrack-tangled, sea's
                  throat hoarse beyond shingle wall,
hand and wrist slipped
   lightly through crook'd arm
      as if belonging-
         such light spaces then-
         till shadows dull
      vacant eyes testing
   marsh horizons...

breakers thud and suck, sky
   shredded with surprised
      flocks, and two pairs
         of eyes prey on tide's offal,
            washed-out footprints, swivel
               to a lone gutted house
               with its absent smoke,
         waders far-off shuttle
      fading further
   as one last fleeting smile
loses its way…

TWO MONTHS APART

As I stack towels to air,
a threadbare, off-white one
slips out, its corner embroidered
Baby in pale gold. Packed off
by you, Mother, to welcome
your autumnal grandchild.
Happy, determined little soul
carried miles north but never
to brighten your shuttered ward.

I wanted you to hold her,
your nursing face tender,
expert with births however hard,
yet delighted by this miracle
as if you'd just performed it.
Would she have charmed you
on your way, or made you
fight more fiercely?

My attempt to bring you back
now feels feeble as this frayed
cotton that served its many bath-times:-
'Nana sent you this before
she died. You were too new
to visit her in hospital.'
I dried her with something
from someone she'd never know
and wrapped her in your love.

NO TIME FOR ROSES

...I'd celebrate the roses of Pæstum that flower twice a year...
      (Virgil: Georgics IV: 119)
...he made for the rose-gardens of sunny Pæstum...
      (Ovid: Metam. XV: 708)
                    ♦

For Ruth, recalling a visit to Castle Howard in 1991
                    ♦

July's claws fix us. Needing a change
from burnt skin and sandy crotches,
we join a glinting cavalcade that rolls
over switchbacks towards the *Great House*,
once founded on trade, now buttressed
by trusts to open as a drive-in shrine.
              Is this where gardens of roses
              burst their buds twice a year?

Obelisk raised to a wily duke's campaigns
and the founder's glorious heritage
parts the straight road. We give way
at gatehouse arches, inhaling velour
and plastic as the 'noble prospect' towers
and expands in a haze of heat and fumes.

Cars graze a flattened paddock. We sweat
in a blazing queue of leisure wear
towards sash-windowed livery stables.
Turnstiles crank us in. *Grounds Only*
for me and my youngest. I'd sag with facts.
She loves space and nosing into flowers.

Not timed past ropes and arrows, pilfered
art, red rooms of state, glass-locked porcelain,
we cross manicured gravel where lord-
and-lady peacocks pick at their demesne.
Ranked limes drench us with shade.
We bathe under canopies of bees and leaves.

Scampering after birds my child leads me
to uncut grass hedged by lopped yews,
dances with butterflies, splashing her summer
stripes round a plinth and urn. I read
HERE A VIRGIL THERE AN OVID
REMEMBER THE ROSES OF PÆSTUM.

Here too a lost son of the house
is mourned and I read from his crumbled
tribute, darkening our talk as we pass
through a thick grove of laurels. Deep
in their shade sculptures pale as new
mushrooms, writhe and leer in twisted postures.

There spreads the south front's ochre mask.
Its fifty steps once fell to four-season
gardens, patterned like a Persian carpet.
Round the Palladian gable triumphal
chariots, banners, plumed helmets moulder
behind moss and scaffold taped red for danger.
                    Where are the gardens of roses
                    that burst their buds again?

ELEGY AT PANTASAPH

For my parents

I pass yew groves and blackened angels
    presiding over Victorian tombs,
cross a bulldozed space where red sorrel
    and speedwell cover the distant dead,
then find them in a suburb of new plots.

A bypass roars like breakers. So many hands
    holding on for dear life.
It shakes me with the stillness of those who rest,
    have no address to find, nowhere
to drive or be driven, their years numbered

in granite. Tribute from a chisel shows
    no more than time served,
when each breath taken and released
    brought changes known only
to those who learned to love against the odds.

These new stones with their gilded screed
    feel like last greetings cards.
They buckle as I say: *sit for ever*
    in easy garden chairs, cats
at your feet, inhaling beds of lavender.

Leave were it not for a brisk
    close-cropped little figure
swathed in fawn. Darts at a headless
    grave, crosses herself, mouths
a prayer, and scuttles off like a leaf.

Pause and calculate. *Sixty-three*
and *sixty-six*. Their score
against mine. A scale to weigh up
chances in this cold spot
without the windbreak they provided.

Bring back their last moments that still
seem the bravest anyone's endured.
Meet the distant stare of mullioned windows.
Look how that dutiful soul
so tightly wrapped jumps into her car.

Soon I follow her along the lime grove
past the closed priory.
Every go-slow hump is someone's grave,
and voices from the rookery
tell me what it's like to survive.

POET IN PERSON

In mem. Anne Beresford

Chairs in a bow window
lit by last sunlight, golden
through autumnal leaves.
A married couple visits
a widow brave in still-raw
singleness. Three picking up
where they left off a year ago.
Are they wiser? Ask that
eye-catching cock pheasant
as it picks through knotted grass.

Their words are the tight embrace
they long to fold her in and make
her world more than a place
of passing light and warmth.

She holds fast to this rambling
damp, pink-rendered house
that lolls on reclaimed marsh among
her reckless shrubs and skyline trees.

Her guests sit down to rich cakes,
and strong tea. The gilded china's
fluted, angular, capacious.
Dusk fills the alcove,
sketches her attentive outline
on the window bench.

She's almost fading to someone
they hope to see, distant friend
who sings in tentative lines
that touch the veins and undersides
of lives, probe the splinters
below our changing skins, light on
corners and crevices to remind us
there are only byways.

APPENDIX & NOTES

Appendix

Author's Comment on aspects of this further edition of the 2009 Collection.

The original proposed title was not *'No Time for Roses'* but *'Heat of the Moment'* since it echoes so many of the poems' themes and occasions, but the editors insisted their suggestion was more 'eye-catching', even though the poem 'No Time for Roses' while vital to the collection's unfolding, does not distil its central 'drive' either in its title or preoccupations.

Interestingly, though, when the collection was first advertised on the Poetry Salzburg website, one of the two poems selected as prime examples of the writing was 'Heat of the Moment'.

Furthermore, Rosemary, my wife, had sketched cover illustrations for both titles. But there was insistence on the use of 'in-house' art, which resulted in an image of a rose emerging from a drain cover. I found this both garish and lacking appropriate 'suggestiveness' for the book's content and focus.

Notes

Inheritance: Page 12:
Sir George Grove (1820-1900) trained as a civil engineer, assisted with railway projects and the construction of Crystal Palace. He later turned his passion for music to producing a *Dictionary of Music and Musicians* (1889) and *Beethoven and his Nine Symphonies* (1896)

Dido & Aeneas: **Page 23:**
1. These haikus reflect on Aeneid I, 749-56, II & IV *passim*, and VI, 440-76.
2. 'Sidonian': term for Dido who escaped to Carthage from the region of Phoenician Tyre/Sidon after the murder of her husband.

A Century on at Aldeburgh: **Page 30:**
A wealthy rationalist banker, Edward Clodd, invited Hardy to house parties of congenial thinkers at his Aldeburgh residence, and in 1909 invited the poet and his new-found companion and admirer, Florence Dugdale, to stay for 10 days. Further regular spring and autumn invitations followed.

Last Testament Too Late: **Page 32:**
Hardy wished to be buried among forebears at Stinsford. His literary executor, Edward Cockerel, decided Westminster Abbey would be more appropriate, and overruled Hardy's wife and family only to be told by the Abbey that space in *Poets' Corner* was so limited that cremation was essential, a further shock to the family. The vicar of Stinsford suggested a repugnant compromise that somehow passed muster: Hardy's heart should be cut out and buried according to his wishes.

Radioactive: **Page 37:**
'Sub-fleet garbage': spent nuclear fuel from submarines dispatched 3000 miles by rail through densely-populated areas to this remote region. The 'pan handle' is a long, narrow fertile area.

The Pool Bethzatha: **Pages 52-3:**
The Jewish authorities banned any exertion on the Sabbath. Even healing was regarded as 'work'. In regarding the sick man and healing him Jesus is felt to be lamenting and repairing the state of his People.

Safely to Piccadilly Station: **Page 65:**
Japamala: a Hindu necklace or set of recitation beads representing the 108 names of God.

9 781835 632628